Unless otherwise noted, all Scripture quotations are taken from the *King James Version of the Holy Bible.*

Scripture quotations marked *Amplified* are taken from *KJV/ Amplified Bible Parallel Edition.* Copyright 1995 by Zondervan.

Scripture quotations marked NKJV are taken from *New King James Version/Giant Print Center Column Reference Edition.* Copyright 1999 by Thomas Nelson Publishers

First Lady: The Real Truth
A Practical Approach to an Ambiguous Role

©2007, 2009, 2024 by Candie A. Price
ISBN 0-9777032-7-4
3rd Edition
Printed in the United States of America

Library of Congress Cataloging-in-Publication Data
First Lady: The Real Truth/Candie Price
Summary: "Explores practical and biblical wisdom for the pastor's wife in today's church." --Provided by Publisher
ISBN: 0-9777032-7-4 (trade cover)

First Lady:
The Real Truth

A Practical Approach to an Ambiguous Role

Candie A. Price

CONTENTS

Dedication

Rev. Arthur Price, Jr.

My beloved partner,

my greatest example,

my best friend.

Like an apple tree among the trees of the woods,
So is my beloved among the sons.
I sat down in his shade with great delight,
And his fruit was sweet to my taste.
Song of Solomon 2:3

Acknowledgements

Surely, I cannot begin to list all of the amazing people that have encouraged me and supported me throughout the preparation and writing of this manuscript. So, to everyone that had a hand in helping me to birth this project, I say a wholehearted and sincere, "Thank You!"

However, there are a few people that I want to personally thank for their awesome love, friendship and prayers:

To Rindia Hunt for her unwavering love: Sister/Friend, Thanks for being my #1 fan and never letting me give up!

To Tamiko Elston, thanks for keeping me focused and pushing me to the finish line!

And a most honorable mention to Mary Betner McLaughlin (my second MOM) and Joanne Newby: My SMBC connection! You are the best friends a sistah could have in her corner!

Thank you to my daughters, Eboni Paige and Amyna Janel for being the coolest daughters I know.

To my publisher/partner/friend, Lisa Benn – There aren't even enough words or space to thank you for your support and friendship – Get those baskets ready – apples are coming!!! YOU are a WOWderful woman!

Last, but not least, to the best example of a pastor's wife, a true and living Proverbs 31 inspiration: Diane H. Gordon - I love you, Sis. G!

Foreword

I have had the opportunity to watch Candie grow into her role as a Pastor's wife. I can still vividly remember her introducing herself at the first Ministers' Wives meeting she attended, "Hi, I'm Candie and I'm pumped!" She has a way of making an impression upon you that you will not soon forget. Candie has allowed the Holy Spirit to season and use her very outgoing and "keeping it real" personality to bless the women of God. That is why I am excited that she has decided to share her insights and experiences in this very candid book on the role of the First Lady.

You will find her insights practical and her transparency not only refreshing, but liberating as she speaks from her own experiences. Candie approaches the subject without pretense or apology as she challenges ministers' wives to grow and flourish in their role. As a Pastor's wife of over twenty years, I found myself remembering and relating. I am sure this book will encourage, challenge and help to liberate you so that you will be an asset and not a liability to your husband and the people you serve.

Diane H. Gordon, First Lady
St. Matthew's Baptist Church
Williamstown, NJ

Introduction

Why write a book about pastor's wives? When the Lord first gave this task to me years ago, there wasn't a whole lot of information out there directed to pastor's wives, although now there is a plethora of information popping up all the time.

I remember the exact point that God spoke to me to write the book. I was at a women's conference and one of the speaker's called all of the pastor's wives to the front to pray for them. We all held hands together as she prayed a fiery prayer on our behalf. I remember her prayer being full of encouragement for the many things that pastor's wives endure – her words spoke directly to my spirit. I was crying and boo-hooing and when she finished, I looked up and the first thing that I noticed was that I was the only one crying! If memory serves me correctly, there were at least three other women standing beside me and not one of them showed any emotion at all! I was baffled! How could they not have felt those words deep into their being??? I recall saying to myself, "Either I'm the only one going through anything or they are very good at faking it!" I realized then that pastor's wives can be masters at putting up facades and hiding pain, as we all do! I wanted to write a book that, although it speaks to those that are already in the position, serves as a reference point for new pastor's/minister's wives and laypeople alike. It's time to shed some light on some of these issues and tell the "real truth."

My first thoughts were to interview as many pastor's/ minister's wives as I possibly could to see what the book should focus on and how I should approach it. I sent out a mass email through my friend, Veda Brown's company, Blackgospelpromo. To my surprise, I received tons of emails and phone calls from women across the country who wanted to share their stories. A lot of them had been through hell and back and they were all excited to see that someone was willing to talk to them about their experiences. This sudden interest in the project, quite frankly, scared me half to death and I became gripped with uncertainty and angst! Maybe I wasn't the one to write this book, I hadn't experienced a lot of the pain and drama that was being expressed to me from a lot of these women. I called my spiritual mom, Mary Bennett McLaughlin, and she prayed with me. She encouraged me not to fear and to do what the Lord had set aside for me to do.

So after about six months of gathering stories from other women via email and phone, some of whom even sent me books about their personal pain, I was ready to write the book. However, my laptop computer crashed, with all the interviews, questionnaires and contact information that I had received – gone! I had no way of knowing with whom I had talked and how to get back in touch with them. Certainly, because of this I believed that I was not to write the book. However, God allowed me to see that it wasn't the testimonies of others that He wanted me to share, it was my own. So the process began for me to seek God about what it was that was to be included in the book. And it all begins with the following questions that each pastor's/minister's wife should ask herself:

Who am I and what do I expect from this position as pastor's/minister's wife? It took me a long time to finally be able to come up with an answer to that question. Ministry has a way of thrusting this question in your face and it is better to know who you are before you get involved than struggling to come up with an answer later. Unfortunately for me, but ultimately by design, I did not find out who I was before I got involved in ministry. My husband, Arthur, and I got married very young. I was 23 and he 24. We dated for seven months, got engaged, and married eight months after that. Six months later he was called to preach. We welcomed our first daughter into our lives two weeks before our second anniversary and three months later we were on our way to Divinity School in upstate New York to prepare my husband for full-time ministry. What a whirlwind of events!

Who was I? A young bride, minister's wife and mother of a three-month old who was now over 500 miles away from her family, friends, and church family and about to journey on the most incredible faith walk she had ever known! Our modest two-income family had turned into a no-income family living in a strange, cold (very cold!), land. Who was I? I hadn't a clue, but I was going to find out soon enough.

How was I supposed to prepare for this life change? I did not recall receiving a handbook when my husband got licensed, I wasn't told to attend any classes, and there were no lectures, conferences or seminars. Where were the older ladies that were supposed to come to your rescue as in Titus 2 and sit you down and "school" you on what was to come? I was waiting for someone to say, "Baby, this is what you need to do…this is what you should prepare for..." And I don't mean the kind of instruction that says, "You need to wear white on first Sunday, sit on the front row and join the deaconess ministry!"

In the midst of all of the fast moving drama that was becoming our life, I had to find out on my own what my role in all of this was and what it all meant. My husband wasn't just preparing to be a minister of the Gospel, he was to become a pastor!

I have always been one of those people who needed to know everything – what are we doing, how are we going to do it and then what? I understand fully the concept of faith and I've been in church long enough to know the lingo, but I still had to know so that I could prepare, adapt and accept, so I thought. Well, God surely has a way of stripping you of your idiosyncrasies. After enough faith tests, your objective is no longer to know what God is doing, but rather to trust in the fact that whatever He is doing it is ultimately for your good and His glory! Romans 8:28

says: [28]And we know that all things work together for good to those who love God, to those who are the called according to *His* purpose. In essence, God has a plan for my life, and no matter what I must go through in the process of that plan coming to fruition, it will ultimately work out for my good because He has ordained it so! It was time to put that scripture to the test and choose to either believe it or not! I had to strip away my desire to know ahead of time what God was doing and rely on the fact that He had everything under control and had my best interest in His heart!

I pray that this book ministers to you and that after you finish meditating on its contents the role of pastor's/minister's wife is a little less ambiguous for you. Remember that God has something so unique for you that He has commissioned it just for you to do – no one else can do what He's ordained just for you. If you don't do it, then you've not fulfilled your purpose. I pray that this is a tool to bring you a little closer to finding and pursuing His purpose for you!

Be encouraged and be blessed!

Candie

FIRST LADY: THE REAL TRUTH

CHAPTER 1

[21]If a man therefore purge himself from these, he shall be a vessel unto honour, sanctified, and meet for the master's use, and prepared unto every good work. II Timothy 2:21

Who are you and what are your expectations?

What exactly do I mean by finding out who you are, and how does one go about doing that? Finding this information out for yourself is crucial. Once you can identify these things for yourself, you can acclimate much easier to your role. If you don't know who you are, you may spend a lot of useless time trying to be to others who you were not meant to be. Before entering the position of a pastor's wife or minister's wife, you must know your place, your purpose, your personality and your passion.

Your Place

For me the word place is not only a positional reference, but it also refers to roles. Positionally you must understand that your place is alongside your husband. You are to be a helpmeet, a supporter, his biggest fan and his own personal exhorter. Ministry is tough! It can sometimes be more brutal than any other line of employment out there. There will be many times when God's people will literally, physically and mentally wear your husband down! It is your role, your responsibility as his mate to encourage, exhort and ease some of the pressures that he faces and/or will face. Now, be careful, don't go up in the church trying to fight all his battles and verse everyone out about how they better back off your husband! The Lord has his back and will handle his adversaries, you only need be prayerful and supportive.

I ad to learn this the hard way. I was straight out of the streets of Philadelphia and dared anyone to say anything about my husband negatively or else it was on! They wouldn't know what hit them after I gave my tongue full reign! But the Lord challenged me to be silent and pray and watch Him move on my husband's behalf and I *learned* to back off. After all, the Lord is the One who called my husband into ministry, surely He could take care of him. Now, I won't try to deny that sometimes that's easier said than done and that I don't still have those times when I want to give some people a serious tongue lashing (ooooh, it's sooo tempting!), but I have to pull myself together and bring my tongue under subjection. I'm to be his covering through my actions, through prayer and by submitting not only to him but also the Holy Spirit! You have to

18

remember it's not your battle, it's the Lord's.

Not only does your place refer to your position next to your husbnd as a supporter, but it also refers to your role as a pastor's or minister's wife. What exactly is that role and who gets to define it?

The first thing you must understand is that you have been called into a very ambiguous position. And yes, I did say you were *called*! My husband is pastoring at his second church and for a second time I've heard, "We didn't call her, we called him!" I even had someone recently tell me, although his intentions were harmless, "We called him, you were drafted!" Many churches believe this wholeheartedly, but it is a wrong interpretation of the pastor's wife's position. No, you were not called to pastor the church, no, you are not making the decisions for the church, but you have been called into a ministry! Although the Bible does not outline specifically the calling and responsibilities of the pastor's wife, it does make mention the importance of the role of women married to men in ministry. The Bible refers to "priests", "prophets" and "deacons" as having specific and important roles in the church, with the moral and spiritual standing of each being similar. Many of these men were not married because of the difficulties they encountered in ministry. However, the women that did marry such men had to exemplify the highest standards of integrity. The Levitical priests were to demonstrate a life of holiness as they represented God to the people, thus, their wives were hand-picked virgins (Lev. 21:7,13). Paul writes to Timothy, a young pastor, and delineates the characteristics and self-control necessary for the wives of spiritual leaders (I Tim. 3:11,12) To be a wife of a spiritual leader is a calling upon your life, given by God! Just as you were called to be in the body of Christ, your marriage, specifically to a man of God, is also a calling, and a very important one to the body of Christ! The role of a pastor's wife is so important that it can make or break a church! I've talked to women across the country about this position and either the pastor's wife is an asset to the ministry or a hindrance!

The Bible says that the two shall become one flesh (Genesis 2:24) – you are joined together as a unit, but with different roles and responsibilities. There is hardly any other position out there where the spouse is looked at as being a major part of her husband's accomplishments or lack thereof than that of the position of the pastor's wife (other than the president of the United States!). If this is true, then how can we continue to look at this position as if it is not one that has been called by God? Is a doctor's wife looked upon when her husband succeeds or fails in surgery? Is the lawyer's wife looked upon when her husband wins or loses a case? No, but rest assure that all eyes are on the pastor's wife as well as on the pastor. Yet, many claim that her life has not been called! You have been called into ministry and your role and responsibilities must be discussed with your spouse. Determine, if possible, BEFORE going into a church what he expects of you and purpose in your heart to fulfill those expectations.

Your Purpose

A part of knowing who you are is knowing what your purpose is and that means the role you will play in your husband's ministry. What are both his and your expectations? Does he even want you involved in the ministry and/or do you even desire to be involved in ministry? There are many pastors who would prefer that heir wives not get involved in ministry at all – some out of pure motives, others with less than pure motives. Whatever the case, you need to know where your spouse stands. Some pastors want to spare their wives from church polity and the many negative aspects of ministry and, therefore, prefer that they not be directly involved in any area of the church. There are others that feel that their wives should only be at the church for their own support and assistance and should not work in the church. And then there are pastors that want their wives to exercise their gifts in the church, whatever they might be. In my opinion, the right way is the way in which the pastor and his wife have discussed works best for their family and their church body. That's why it is so important that these expectations and desires be discussed before going into a church or soon after determining what the needs of that congregation are. Don't expect or allow the church itself to call the shots on what roles and responsibilities you should hold. Only the Lord, your husband, and you can make that judgment call.

The church might have a role prepared for you that is totally not designed or God-ordained for you and that will set you up for a complete failure. As Christians we must operate within our own gifts and if you find yourself with a gift that is not being accepted or appreciated, stand still, pray and wait until the Lord opens the door for your gift to be utilized. You'll either find out that it's not your time or that it wasn't really *your* gift. You might be a wife to a husband who forbids that you operate within the gift you feel you have, or even a wife of a husband that is pushing you into a gift that you feel is not where God wants you. After discussing this situation with him and he does not hear, you must earnestly pray and turn it over to the Lord and wait until He answers. In the meantime, what is the Lord trying to get out of you? What area in your life is He trying to prune? Is it patience? Is it perseverance? Is it submission? There is always a lesson to be learned from our trials and circumstances. Seek God's face and earnestly discover what He is trying to show you through your situation. In essence, seek wisdom while waiting!

Years ago, I can recall going to Sunday School class and feeling so dissatisfied with the person who was teaching. It wasn't that I wanted to teach the class and felt that I would be better at it, because I didn't (although I knew that teaching was one of my gifts). I just wanted him to study so that he could provide sound instruction to the students, most of whom were new to systematic Bible study. I would leave Sunday School every Sunday frustrated! I didn't want to keep interjecting with important points because I didn't want him to feel that I was trying to take over his class, but I also didn't want the students to go away without a more in-depth examination of God's Word. I have to admit it was a very awkward time and most times I had to just pray and suck it up! He continued to teach, but what was funny was that after a while he had gotten to the point where he would say, "Is that right, Sis. Price?" I didn't want him to feel the need to get my approval – after all it's God who is holding us accountable, but at least it meant to me that he knew he had to study before standing in front of the class. I probably could have taught that class better than he, but it wasn't about who could teach the best! We don't have to force our gifts on anyone, we have to look at what the overall objective is: to win souls, to edify the saints, and to exalt the Lord Jesus! As a pastor's wife you have to be able to handle those sticky situations with patience and tact. I could have made the situation worse if I had tried to push my knowledge above that of the teacher's or make him feel inadequate. Make sure that you and your spouse have conversations about what is expected of you and what you, yourself, expect so that when situations like these come up, you know your place and your purpose.

Your Personality

This is surely a topic that I'm all too familiar with! A major part of knowing yourself is understanding your own personality.

Are you an introvert, extrovert, sensitive or intuitive? Are you a thinker or a feeler, do you judge or perceive? Why is this important? Suppose you are an introvert and extremely private and your spouse is an extrovert, extremely charismatic and appealing.

People are drawn to him like a moth to a flame, yet you don't really care to be around a lot of people. How will you handle this dichotomy? People will, undoubtedly, perceive that he is friendly, and you are not, even if that is not really the case. Suppose you are very intuitive and cautious and are a person that prefers to listen rather than talk, always careful about choosing your words – will others perceive you as being non-approachable and distant? Let's face it, ladies, no matter what your personality, people will have something to say about it, but it's important that you analyze yourself and be aware of what your challenges may or may not be beforehand.

There is also the perception out there somewhere in fantasy land that pastor's wives ought to be and look a certain way. Although none of these expectations are grounded in any biblical notation, they are, nonetheless, thought to be a universal sign of a pastor's wife. I can't tell you how many times a visiting pastor and his wife have come to our church or we would go to a visiting church, and someone else would be mistaken for my husband's wife. The women they mistook for me, more often than not, were wearing a big hat, were older than I and had on what we used to call " Sunday go-to-meeting clothes!" I, on the other hand, might show up with braids in my hair, very modern attire, and not look at all like the "pastor's wife" –whatever that is. My point is that you have to know what the expectations or assumptions about your position are, and if your tastes and your personality differ from them, be prepared to deal with that.

What if your personality gets in the way of your husband's ministry? Suppose you are an extreme extrovert, very outgoing, very outspoken, yet your husband would rather you tone it down a notch and not be YOU so much in the church. What if you are extremely shy and your husband would like you to interact more with the saints? How do you handle it when your personality is conflicting with his goals? Do you stick to your guns and say "Well, that's just me!" or do you try to identify a healthy balance so that you cannot only be yourself, but also be an asset to his ministry as well?

One of the best pieces of advice I have ever gotten was from my own first lady, Diane Gordon, from St. Matthew's Baptist Church in Williamstown, NJ. She said, "Candie, you have to be willing to give God permission to change your personality!" That was a profound moment for me because I had come to know some things about myself: I'm personable, outgoing and outspoken, but I can be abrasively honest and quick tongued. Are all of these aspects of my personality in line with what God wants and will they be an asset or a hindrance to my husband's ministry? If not, then I must be willing to allow God to change whatever He needs to in me so that when people see me they no longer see Candie (or at least a lot less Candie, I'm still a work in progress) but that they see the Christ that dwelleth in me!

List your personality traits, even the ugly ones and then analyze whether they are assets to God and assets to your husband's ministry. Don't worry about the expectations of the masses and what they think you ought to look like or how you ought to behave. They will always have an opinion either way. Always remember the ultimate goal: to be a vessel of honor to the Lord and not a useless cistern!

Your Passion

What area of ministry are you passionate about, if any? This will help you and your spouse determine what area of his ministry you will be an asset to. Is it working with the youth, or women's ministry? Is it being in a visible position or do you prefer the background? There is also the possibility that you don't desire to work in any area of the church but would rather just be an intercessor for your spouse as he ministers. Don't feel as if you have to be involved in the ministry and don't compare yourself with other pastor's wives and what they're doing or not doing! Often times we embrace those fantasy land expectations that we talked about earlier and feel that we must fit the mold that others have made for us. All pastor's wives don't work with the children's ministry! All pastor's wives don't just sit and look pretty. All pastor's wives are not active, and all pastor's wives are not passive! If you get anything from this book, please get this: find out who you are, what God's plan for you is, what your husband expects, what you expect, and work within those parameters!

Prayer: *Lord, I understand that my role as a pastor's/ minister's wife will be filled with many challenges. Help me to discover who I am in you, what purpose you have for my life, and determine what my expectations and my spouse's expectations are. Above all else, I want to be a vessel of honor, fit for your use and prepared unto every good work! Amen.*

FIRST LADY: THE REAL TRUTH

CHAPTER 2

"But she who is married cares about the things of the world— how she may please her husband." I Corinthians 7:34

We are family: Developing closeness at home

Ministry can take a toll on the relationship between a pastor and his wife. Just think about it. most pastors spend an enormous time at the church, in meetings, visiting the sick and bereaved, preparing and studying God's Word, along with other countless duties. How do you balance those schedules in addition to those of your children and yourself? It's not easy by any means, but it is important and necessary for you and your spouse to carve out quality time for one another and develop closeness in the home.

Satan will always be looking for a way to come between

the man of God and his wife. He knows full well the value of the job that lay before both of you. Our Lord said it best when He told Peter, "Simon, Simon, behold, Satan hath desired *to have* you, that he may sift *you* as wheat: [32]But I have prayed for thee, that thy faith fail not." (Luke 22:30-31) In that sifting process Satan wants to shake up your marriage, your mindset and your ministry! Your objective should be to set up a line of defense that is impenetrable so that when the attacks on your family and ministry come from the outside (and they will come!), they don't affect what goes on between the two of you on the inside. Above all, remember that Jesus, himself prayed for us and is constantly making intercession on our behalf! He knows everything there is to know about you – your struggles, your frustrations, your pain and He's already made provision for you to be victorious!

It is a given that we will all experience some rocky times in our marriages - that goes with the territory when two attempt to become one flesh but add to that the stress and responsibilities of a ministry and, if not properly handled, those rocky times can turn catastrophic. How then do you make sure that your home-life is such that it is not affected by the ministry or have an adverse effect on the ministry? Communication, commitment, and compromise.

Communication

A lack of communication can destroy any marriage! How many times have you had arguments or disagreements in your marriage simply because of miscommunication? Miscommunication is an effective tool that the devil uses to bring division! If it weren't so effective, we might have a much lower rate of divorce in our society. That's why it is so important to discuss openly what's going on with you and your spouse. Don't leave issues open ended, don't allow silence to kill your closeness. The silent treatment is never an appropriate response to conflict, and neither is this dialogue:

Spouse: What's the matter?

You: Nothing.

Spouse: Are you sure, it seems like something's the matter.

You: I said nothing.

Spouse: Okay.

Then he goes about his business, and you get mad because he didn't keep hammering you until he got it out of you! Don't play the Nothing's Wrong Game, it really isn't a truthful approach, and it won't solve a thing!

Pastor's wives are put a in a very precarious position. We are not only under our husband's leadership in the home, but also in the church. And for the pastor's wife who works at the church – she has to submit to his leadership at home, in the church, and at work! How do you balance all of that and how do you effectively communicate conflict when he's the authority everywhere, it seems?

Well, there's this six-letter word out there that seems to scare the dickens out of every Christian woman, but we can't get away from it! Are you ready? Here goes......SUBMIT!

I know, you didn't want to hear that word and probably thought you'd get through the entire book without hearing it! Sorry. It must be said. In order to effectively communicate, in order to balance all of those areas in which your husband is leading – you have to be submissive. Not just to your spouse, but more importantly to the Holy Spirit! If you are not under the guidance and leading of the Holy Spirit in your daily walk with the Lord, you are going to have major problems in your home and in your relationship with your spouse! Remember that submission is an act of your will (I Peter 3:1)! You must allow your spouse to lead your family and his congregation in the way that he feels led through the power of the Holy Spirit. If there are areas in his leadership that are faulty or out of God's will, if you feel you cannot communicate those thoughts with him directly, then you have to do as my husband always says, "If you can't talk to the person, talk to God about the person!" If your husband's desire is to be pleasing to the Lord, the Lord will reveal to him those things you could not.

Tighten up your communication. Make talking to you easy. He should feel that he can come to you with anything, and you are there and willing to listen. My husband always comes to me with his sermon ideas. To be honest, I don't always want to hear them, especially if my mind is somewhere else– it's "preacher talk" that sometimes I feel he should be sharing with his preacher friends.

But I am there for him and interested in what he has to say and want him to know that he can always share those thoughts with me. A lot of times I help him work through some things, and that's a very satisfying feeling. Share your day with him, whether you are a working woman or a stay-at-home mother, keep one another informed of what's going on in your life. Carve out regular time to talk. My husband and I love to sit at the table over a cup of coffee and talk. We talk in the car, we talk in the bed, and if we're not talking…something is wrong!

Talk about more than just church! We have to keep a balance in our lives, and we have to understand that our marriage should not be consumed by "church stuff". Communicate your collective goals for your marriage and your future. If you are working, what are your plans and goals? How will both of your job goals fit together? What will you do when and if he decides to retire? Approximately when would he like to retire? If you are living away from your hometown, will you remain there in retirement or will you move back home? What will you do when the kids are gone? What types of places would you like to visit? God has given you a marriage – a wonderful gift and time for you to share your lives together. Make it a full and prosperous life – well balanced and free of miscommunication.

A word to the wise: keep the major things between you at home! Never, ever, ever bring them into the church. The congregation should never know when the two of you are disagreeing or having trouble – it's not the place to air your laundry! I'm not talking about if your husband uses glimpses of your life as an example to share with others during his sermons – It's like that Vegas commercial – what goes on in Vegas stays in Vegas – if you and your spouse are disagreeing then what goes on in your household stays in your household. Which brings up another point: what if your husband shares information about your private life that you would rather he didn't? Don't show your disgust in the middle of the service! Talk to him at home about how it makes you feel if you are uneasy and work it out between the two of you. Personally, I have never been bothered by my husband's examples about our lives. I am an open person, for the most part, and I believe that people can relate practical truths to personal stories. However, there was this one time.....

Years ago my husband and I got up one Sunday and prepared for church, as usual. Somehow, we got into a disagreement, which is a very rare occurrence on a Sunday morning. I couldn't even tell you what the disagreement was about but I just remembered he was wrong and I was right! (smile) He preached that Sunday and after his sermon he alluded to the fact that he had done something and needed to make an apology. He called me up to the front of the church and apologized in front of the congregation. I was livid and very embarrassed! I did the "first lady smile" and sat down in my seat, but when we got home I asked him very politely (or as politely as I could!) to never do that again and shared my feelings and frustration, and not to mention the possible repercussions of such an action. The lives of a pastor and his wife are always under the microscope as it is – people are always judging you and watching how you interact with one another – do you really want to add more attention to yourselves by allowing them into your disagreements as well? He listened to my reasoning and we worked through that issue together. Even well intentioned, Spirit-filled pastors make mistakes!! We must be willing to be honest with one another and work through our differences or Satan will claim a foothold and decide to stay a while!

Commitment

If you're going to have closeness in your relationship with one another you must have commitment. You both must be committed to making your marriage a priority, above ministry, and taking the time to cultivating it and making it work. Yes, I said above ministry. Your husband's first ministry is to you and not the church, and vice versa. The order should be Christ first, spouse/family second, ministry third. That is the proper order for anyone in ministry! I remember my pastor, Dr. Raymond Gordon, saying often, "If you're down here at the church every day – then you're running from something at home!" He made a point to instruct those in ministry that their time with their family was very important and that balance was not an option but a necessity.

So often we hear of pastors who have jumped headfirst into ministry taking time from their families consistently and often leaving their wives feeling alone and rejected. Some women don't worry about other women taking their husband away – they feel that the church is the other woman! If this is your story, you must express your concerns and sit down with your spouse to have a genuine dialogue about how much time spent at the church is reasonable.

I think that all pastor's wives have struggled with this area at one time or another. When my husband was first called to a church, we talked extensively about the time we would allot to ministry and the time that was "our time". It just so happened that Arthur's time at church didn't intrude on our family time because the church was very small. We were able to make family time for ourselves and our two small daughters. Every Friday night we did something with the girls – be it going to the mall, movies or playing games in the house. Saturday was also set aside as our day! My husband did not allow any meetings to be scheduled on Saturday. My girls and I knew that Saturday morning and Saturday afternoon up until about 3:00 or 4:00 p.m. we had my husband to ourselves before he would have to get home and put the finishing touches on his sermon. We often took trips to Niagara Falls or went to Canada for a day to get away. My most frustrating times seemed to be right after church on Sundays. I would get so aggravated because that was the time people chose to hold long conversations with him and require his attention. I was ready to go! I felt that since he had been in the office all week, (and my husband is a workaholic so he hardly EVER took time off!!) taught

Bible Study on Wednesday, came to trustee and deacon meetings –
then they ought not stop him on Sunday afternoon after he had just
finished preaching his head off!! Let the man go – we've got to go
eat!!!

I'm sure there are many of you shaking your heads right
now because you can relate to that scenario. I really struggled with
that resentment for a while until I just asked God to give me a little
more patience. Arthur is a great husband; he is a great father. He
spends as much time with us as is humanly possible, but he is also
a great pastor! He would never turn a member away. He is always
there to listen and to help and I wouldn't have it any other way!
So, I began to thank God for making him such an awesome leader
both in the home and in the church and I just became a little more
patient.

Now, don't think I still don't struggle with wanting him to
myself. That's a reality for any wife! Our present church is larger
than the previous one and his responsibilities have at least tripled.
But he still spends as much time with us as is possible and he's
still a great pastor! I want desperately to suck my teeth sometimes
when he has to go do something at church, but then I remember
that patience I asked for and the thankful heart I have for such a
wonderful man!

Make the commitment to ironing out the snags and the
little things that can come up to irritate you and get you both
off track. Make the commitment not to let anything or anyone

37

come between you. Don't allow others to come to you with junk about your spouse. Always, always give him the benefit of the doubt and when in doubt ask! And when you ask, ask in love and not accusation. Remember that this is the man you agreed to be united with as you stood in front of all those well-dressed people and spent all that money. Respect him, reverence him and be committed to him.

Compromise

There has to be some compromise, or things will go awry very quickly! As your husband enters into the lifestyle of a pastor, you must understand that there will be times when you and he will have to make concessions for the other so that there is peace in the home. Whatever your issues are, make sure that you both understand that to make any marriage work, you must be willing to listen and to compromise.

What if he is not willing to compromise? What if he insists that only the things that he does are important? What if he feels that his ministry supersedes yours or that your jobs, be they inside or outside the house, are not as important? What if you feel like you have communicated and committed and compromised enough yet he hasn't budged? These may be valid feelings. There are many pastors' wives who are frustrated with their spouses because of his failure to compromise. What does God require from us when our spouse is not willing to bend? He requires obedience and consecration.

Obedience

Obedience to what? To His Word. I Peter 3:1 says, [1]Likewise, ye wives, *be* in subjection to your own husbands; that, if any obey not the word, they also may without the word be won by the conversation of the wives; [2]While they behold your chaste conversation *coupled* with fear.

Although this reference specifically concerns the relationship between a saved woman and her unsaved spouse, it is still applicable for a woman whose husband is being disobedient in a certain area of his life. We will discuss this in greater detail later in the book. However, what can be gleaned from this verse for you is that your response to such treatment is to win him by your conversation (behavior). As he "beholds your chaste conversation coupled with fear (respect)" it will prompt him to see his faulty behavior. I'm sure you know by now that you don't have the power to change your husband! Only God can change him so your efforts will be futile if you continue to try! It might seem like you are being called to suffer through this situation, and you are, for such a time as this. Christ was the Suffering Servant and His suffering brought healing to the masses. There is an old saying that says that either we are suffering for a cause or suffering because. We can suffer for the cause of Christ, which will bring healing, or we will suffer because of consequences we must pay because of our actions. Choose the former so that God can get the glory out of your life and bring healing to your spouse rather than making the situation worse by responding in an ungodly manner.

Consecration

Consecrate yourself to prayer and looking like the image of God while you wait for the situation to change. You cannot throw temper tantrums, demand that he yields to your desires, or refuse sexual intimacy until he "gets himself together." God is requiring you to be humble and gentle and to watch Him come to your defense. In the meantime, allow Him to do the work in your husband that He is trying to produce in him. If your husband is a man of God who truly trusts Him and wants to please Him, he already knows what the Word says. He knows God's plan for marriage, and he understands that God requires the husband to give honor to his wife, as the weaker vessel, so that his prayers will not be hindered (I Peter 3:7). Pray and ask God to reveal those truths not just to his head but in his heart!

Making Home a Haven

One thing I like to tell new minister's/pastor's wives is to make sure that your home is a haven for your spouse. He has to deal with a lot of things concerning church business, church people, and the Word of God that he must deliver to the congregation. Make sure that when he comes home, he is coming into a peaceful and loving atmosphere. Make sure that your children know what is required of them during their father's study/ prayer time. Make sure that you also abide by those requirements. Studying the Word is the most important aspect of the pastor's work, so you must not allow anything to interfere with that process. Arthur has a room downstairs all to himself that he can go in and shut the door and we know that he is studying.

If you know in advance what his study habits and "God-time" are, then you can adapt and make plans around that. Don't wait until he's studying to ask him something you could wait for or to "express your feelings!" That's not the time to do it! Be mindful of one another's responsibilities outside the home and make concessions for them.

The last five years of our lives I have been pursuing a college degree and recently graduated. I have to say, it wasn't easy going back to school after all these years, being in the classroom with what I like to call "babies," being the wife of a pastor, raising two children, teaching Sunday School, directing the women's ministry and editing a magazine! It was absolute craziness! But the wonderful part of it all was that although my husband has a very demanding schedule of his own, he helped in every way he possibly could. We shared the responsibilities of the household chores: laundry, dinner, etc. We took turns driving (yes, this pastor's family has only one car!) – depending upon our schedules we determined who would drive when there were conflicts and appointments, etc. We both compromised and made it work, and it did!   He, in turn, also respected the fact that there were times that I had to study, write papers, or meet with group members on a project.

Developing balance in the home and maintaining a peaceful atmosphere can be accomplished. Remember that it takes work, in addition to communication, commitment, and compromise!

Prayer: *Lord, I thank you for the family you have given me. I thank you for this wonderful man of God that you have placed as leader in our home and in our church. Help us to develop a balance in our home as we deal with the pressures of work and responsibilities. Teach us how to communicate and stay committed to one another. Help us to be open to compromise and to not allow outside influences to come between us. We truly want our marriage to reflect your grace and awesome power and the love you have for the Church. Amen.*

FIRST LADY: THE REAL TRUTH

CHAPTER 3

⁴one who rules his own house well, having his children in submission with all reverence ⁵(for if a man does not know how to rule his own house, how will he take care of the church of God?). I Timothy 3:4,5

Adaptation: Helping children adapt to the lifestyle of the pastor's family

We hear it all the time: "The pastor's kids are often the worst kids". Why do you think that is? I've thought about it long and hard because I didn't want my children to be thought of in that way. Although I understand that you can do all you can for your children: raise them in a loving, Christian environment, enroll them in the best schools, give them attention and direction and they can still turn out totally opposite of what you have prepared for them. I think it's very important that we realize that our children are a gift from the Lord, and we have a responsibility to raise them in the fear and admonition of the Lord, regardless of whether they are pastor's kids or not! The Bible gives us clear mandates on child raising: Proverbs 22:6 says to [6]Train up a child in the way he should go: and when he is old, he will not depart from it. After we have done that, it's out of our hands. Pastor Gordon did an awesome series on the family which outlined what we must teach our children: Respect, Restraint and Responsibility. We must teach our children to respect us, their parents, and any other authority figure that stands before them. They will always have authority figures – be they teachers, employers, police officers! We must develop respect in them at an early age so that they understand what is expected of them and become productive citizens at home, in the workplace and in society at large.

We must teach them the parameters of restraint. We cannot always do what we want and have no limitations. Yes, we all have had to deal with hormones, desires and wants but we must understand that there are limits to what we should act on and God's Word must always be the guideline for those restraints. They should know what God says about sex, dating relationships, marriage, work ethics, peer pressure, homosexuality, and all other subjects that they will be introduced to. We, as Christian parents, should not allow the world to dictate to our children how they ought to live. We should set the parameters and the examples.

Our children should have responsibilities. They should know that they must work hard to achieve success and that nothing will be handed to them without merit. They should not always have the latest clothes and gadgets: the iPods, the X-boxes, etc. without having first proved an age-appropriate level of responsibility and good character. Much of the time we give lavishly because we feel guilty about the lack of time we spend with our children. If this is your case, then stop spending money and start spending time!

I recall for the longest time that my children were satisfied with the latest toys from McDonald's! My husband and I didn't lavish them with a lot of toys and gifts when they were younger. Now, I am so grateful that we didn't. They are two of the most appreciative girls when it comes to receiving gifts and they don't ask for everything they see. We have taught them the value of things and they will even respond by saying, "That's too high! That's way too much money for that!" (especially when they have to use their own money to get it!") They may call us cheap from time to time, but they get the point!

These areas of child rearing are important for any child, but let's look at how the pastor's children's lives are different from that of their peers and their friends in the congregation.

The pastor's children will understand early that their lives are different. Their family is always under a microscope, and they might even hear negative things about you and your spouse. Mothers are natural protectors of their children and in this case, it will be no different. It is our responsibility to protect them from negative influences and people. If that means saying no to a person who has invited your children to their house, and you know that they have a history of causing division in the church – then the answer is no! We are very protective of our children, and we don't allow them to visit a lot of folks – and that's people both inside and outside the church. Use discernment – everyone doesn't have the best interest of your family at heart!

The pastor and his wife should discuss early on how they will raise their children and how to best acclimate them into the pastor's lifestyle. What will you tell them if they hear negative discussions? You must think about it before it happens so that you don't respond out of anger and say something you can't take back. Your goal is to always provide for them a godly, but realistic example for them to learn and grow from. Am I saying never to let your children see that you're angry? No, that's unrealistic and certainly not healthy for them in the long run. However, you should have a plan of action as to how you are going to deal with certain issues should they arise.

Does your husband travel a lot for revivals and conferences? You must explain these absences to your children. Be careful not to sound resentful in the presence of your children, they will pick up on that and will adopt that attitude as well. If your husband's schedule bothers you, don't forget the three c's : communication, commitment and compromise. Also make a point to plan for special blocks of time upon his return so that the children feel that they are just as important to him as the people he ministers to.

Another thing we made a point to discuss early on with

our children was that we wanted them to have the most "normal" childhood that they could have. We did not feel the need to make them go down to the church for "everything, every time the doors opened." We did not force them on the choir, auxiliaries, etc. And yes, you will get pressure from ministry leaders who feel that the pastor's kids must participate in everything. We decided that it was important for our children to make those decisions on their own – their lives already centered around the church enough, in our opinion. Eboni, my oldest daughter is pretty laid back. She never wanted to be an usher, she will sing on the choir, but don't expect that she will volunteer for a whole lot. My youngest daughter, Amyna, is the crème d' la crème of personality! When she was younger, she would sign up for just about everything. But we gave them freedom to come to those decisions on their own.

You and your spouse have to decide how you will handle these issues with your children. However, make sure that you are both on the same page and that you present a united front before your children and the congregation.

Talk to your children. Gone are the days when children are just seen and not heard. They have a lot to say. Listen and counsel. Have open discussions about all types of things. I believe in turning almost everything into a lesson. My daughter, Eboni, teases me all the time: "Here you go turning something into a lesson," she says. Well, it's true, but she knows she appreciates it, and she will appreciate it more when she's on her own.

Make sure that your children are guarded with the Word of God. Teach them the Word, have family devotions. Don't just let them get the Word on Sunday. Make sure that they have devotions on their own. There are plenty of good devotionals in the Christian bookstores, buy one and let them have devotions together. Encourage them to have a relationship with Jesus Christ, not just to be church goers.

I believe that's where pastor's and their wives fail their children. They take them to church, they do ministry in church, but they don't teach them to have a relationship with Jesus Christ. It has to be personal to them and not just seen as a part of your job! Some of my friends are pastor's kids and they are just now systematically studying and learning the Word of God and their fathers were pastors for decades!

I am determined that when my children leave my house to go away to college that they will be equipped with God's Word. What they do with it is beyond my control, but I would just fall under a rock if a child that has lived under my roof will go off into the world and not know the Word of God. If the man of God can't rule his own house with the Word of God, how can he be effective in God's house? And the same applies to all of us!

Understand that your children will like some things that you are not totally comfortable with. I don't like rap music, I don't allow rap music to be loudly displayed in my home, however, I'm not stupid! I know my children know who all the latest rappers are and I'm sure they are familiar with all the latest music. They are in school all day long – more than they are at home. And don't think because your child goes to a Christian school that he or she doesn't know the latest trends out there! They know!!! And you've got to come to grips with the fact that they know! We never told our children that they couldn't listen to rap, but they do know where we stand on much of today's music, especially with lyrics containing profanity and explicit language and we neither buy it nor allow it to be brought into the home. I was proud when Eboni came to me and asked me, "Mom, what's wrong with rap music?" We then began a discussion about the music, the lyrics, the message and the witness of rap music and other derogatory music. Of course, we know that all rap music is not bad, but I told her to think about it for herself. The beat aside (because you know they always say the beat is what draws them!), what messages are being conveyed and do these messages conflict with who you say you are in Christ? It was something for her to think about and she thanked me for the discussion. Don't give your kids all the answers, let them think and figure things out for themselves. Will you always be there with them? No, there will be times when they have to go it alone. Just make sure that you and your spouse have given them the tools necessary to make informative and thoughtful choices.

Don't go about setting all these rules and regulations for them to abide by so that they don't experience anything and then when they get from under your thumb, they go what I like to call "buck wild". You can't shield them from everything! You have to be open to discuss things. Just because you don't discuss them doesn't mean they are non-existent. Talk about sex! Talk about dating! Talk about drugs! Talk about partying and clubs and disease! If you don't, they will have to rely on the information from someone else. Do you really want that? The pastor's kids are not exempt from these topics. Don't be so caught up in ministering to God's people and trying to save the world that you forget the most important people that God has given you to minister to: your children!

Prayer: *Heavenly Father, we thank you for the children that you have blessed us with and we understand the mandate to train them up according to your Word and your way. Help us to instill in them respect, restraint and responsibility and to arm them with the Word of God so that they can make godly decisions. We know that being pastor's kids can be a very awkward existence for them in today's society, but we trust that you are leading and directing their lives according to your will for them. Help us not to be so preoccupied with church work that we forget to minister to the needs of our children. Amen.*

FIRST LADY: THE REAL TRUTH

CHAPTER 4

¹Now the LORD had said unto Abram, Get thee out of thy country, and from thy kindred, and from thy father's house, unto a land that I will shew thee .⁵And Abram took Sarai his wife, and Lot his brother's son, and all their substance that they had gathered, and the souls that they had gotten in Haran; and they went forth to go into the land of Canaan; and into the land of Canaan they came. ⁶And Abram passed through the land unto the place of Sichem, unto the plain of Moreh. ¹⁰And there was a famine in the land: and Abram went down into Egypt to sojourn there; for the famine was grievous in the land. ¹And Abram went up out of Egypt, he, and his wife, and all that he had, and Lot with him, into the south. ¹⁸Then Abram removed his tent, and came and dwelt in the plain of Mamre, which is in Hebron, and built there an altar unto the LORD.

Genesis 12:1,5-6, 10; Genesis 13:1, 13

Following the yellow brick road
to the golden path of ministry

I can certainly relate to Abraham's wife, Sarah, as she sojourned with her husband from place to place to place. The Bible doesn't say that she resisted him or doubted his actions like Lot's wife did in Genesis 19. Instead, she trusted in the decisions of both God and her husband as they traveled toward the unknown.

It might be your plight to follow your spouse to reside in a place you've never been before. All of us don't get the opportunity to serve churches that are in proximity of our family and friend connections. The big question is: "If you are called to serve a church far from your family and friends, how will you adjust and adapt?"

In my opinion, this is one of the biggest sacrifices of the

pastor and his family. It is not easy to leave your family, friends, and everything you've ever known to go to another place and live among people you don't know.

The reason I titled this chapter Following the Yellow Brick Road to the Golden Path of Ministry is to alert you to the possibility of packing up everything and leaving the familiar for the unfamiliar and the truth of what might be involved in this process. Understanding what really takes place when you begin this journey, should it become your reality, may save you a lot of grief and disappointment.

When my husband was contemplating going into seminary after the birth of our daughter, I have to say that I was behind him one hundred percent (and he never lets me forget it!). I was the encouraging wife, his greatest fan. I believed that he could do anything he wanted to do and be successful as long as he put his trust in the Lord. Although this was the truth, I now admit that I was very young and full of naiveté. I hadn't really counted the cost to our family, and I hadn't really examined all of the pros and cons and the insurmountable obstacles that would surely come. I had in my mind that we were traveling the yellow brick road of ministry! My husband would go to school, he would learn all he could and when he graduated, he would get a church and we would be involved in ministry! No matter what would come our way, we would make it because our motives were pure, and we had each other! Right? Well, I am here to testify that there is NO such thing as a yellow brick road to ministry and there is certainly no golden path!

It didn't' take long for me to realize that I wasn't prepared for this new journey in our lives. We left our hometown of Philadelphia for Colgate Rochester Divinity School in Rochester, New York in August of 1992. Eboni was three months old and had never been in the care of anyone else but my husband and me. We had no income and the only people we knew were Eboni's godparents, also from Philly, who had been living in Rochester for several years and were waiting to be called to a church. We moved into campus housing and began to settle into our new lives. Well, by November I was fit to be tied and wanted OUT!!!! Rochester was cold and produced more snow than I had ever seen in my entire life! I quickly accumulated a list of cons that literally began to show on my face! 1) I hated cold weather, 2) I didn't know anyone, 3) I couldn't get a job because I couldn't afford daycare and I couldn't leave my baby with just anyone, 4) I felt isolated and alone, 5) did I mention I hated cold weather?

In November the school gave a week off for reading week and most people were going to go home to be with their families to enjoy the Thanksgiving break. It was a six-hour drive from Rochester to Philadelphia and there was a lot of snow on the ground, but I begged Arthur for about a week straight to "TAKE ME HOME!!!!"

In my heart I knew that he was doing the right thing – that God had called him on this journey, but it took a long time for me to adjust to this new lifestyle. We found a church to worship in and the Lord moved me from fear to faith. I will say that the members of Mt. Vernon Baptist Church in Rochester, NY were the angels that the Lord sent to us to assist us during those difficult times. They welcomed us, they nurtured us, and they accepted us into their homes and into their lives. They gave us a sense of community and family which made our existence away from home a lot more palatable. We will be eternally grateful to Deloris Ford, Doddie and Wayne Franklin, and Nancy and Nate McFarland, among others, who believed in our commitment to God's plan for us and encouraged and supported us physically, spiritually, and financially.

However, those times of uncertainty and disconnection would return as we moved again to Buffalo and then to Birmingham. How do you deal with moving your entire family in order to serve God's people? How do you cope with the isolation and the loneliness? Faith, fervor and friendships.

Faith

It takes enormous faith to leave everything you've known for the uncertain. But isn't that what Christians do when they leave behind their old lifestyles for a new life in Christ? We have to trust that God has our back and that if He is leading us He has our future under total control. Hebrews 11 outlines for us the many testimonies of those in the Bible that stepped out on faith and watched as God delivered them from their circumstances and afflictions. Chapter 12 begins by telling us that because of these witnesses, we, too, can lay aside every weight and the sin of doubt that so easily embraces us! We truly can do all things through Christ that strengthens us, but we must have faith.

It is not easy to do, but if you and your family are called away to what seems a "strange land" to do ministry, know that you can overcome the obstacles that Satan will send and that you are more than a conqueror through Jesus Christ. God is not a man that He should lie and He will supply ALL your need according to His riches in glory!

The best advice I could give you is to make sure that you and your spouse sit down and explore all of the pros and cons of the ministry and how it will impact your lives. Going into this life with a clear picture of how it will affect you will be the best preparation you can make for a successful ministry and marriage.

Fervor

Bring with you to your new surroundings the fervor and zeal that God has placed within you concerning ministry. Whatever your part is to be in the church, whether it be as a leader or not, purpose in your heart to remain focused and vigilant to the task.

Satan will try so many times and in so many ways to get you unraveled and unfocused. He will try to distract you by comparing your lifestyle to that of other pastors and their families. He will try to make you feel inadequate and "wrong" for the part and ready to give up at the first sign of trouble. But know that God has already made a way for you to be successful. No, its not a "golden path" but it is the path that He has preordained just for you! Walk the path He has for you with diligence and fervor!

Friendships

The life of a pastor's/minister's wife can be very lonely and isolated. But it doesn't have to be. There is an awkward stage at the beginning of every new pastorate where the people are feeling him out and he is feeling them out as well. But don't forget, they've got their eyes on you, too. As a result, they will appear to be very friendly or very distant. They will seem to embrace you or ignore you. This is natural because they don't know you and you don't know them. They don't know what type of "pastor's wife" you'll be. Remember, they already have their own preconceived notions about how you *should* be, so they are trying to see if you fit their expectations.

For some pastor's wives this awkward stage seems an eternity. You are already missing home, away from your comfort zone, having to learn a new city and new surroundings, and then you are either treated like you don't exist or are under constant watch. Be patient and pray. Pray for your husband, pray for the congregation and pray for yourself! If you think it's hard to put two people together and make them one, try the marriage between the pastor, his family and a church!

Before every big move we've made I've asked the Lord to send me people I can trust, people I can be myself around and He's done that consistently for me. I am an outgoing person (to an extent) in that I love to fellowship with others. Maybe because I am an only child I have the need to be in intimate fellowships with others. I don't like large crowds, but a small group is just up my alley! It's very hard to have close relationships with people within the congregation because you don't know who you can trust. Let's face it, everyone in the church does not have your best interest at heart and some are just outright deceptive. But ask God to reveal to you, early on, who is sincere and who is not. Be wise in your selections, always praying and asking God to weed out any toxic individuals (and He will do this as well!). Look for the type of people that will accept you as you are, but that will also pray for and with you to become all that God has for you to become. Pray for individuals who will hold you accountable and whose tongues are uplifting and edifying. Pray for individuals for whom you can be a positive influence and mentor. Pray for relationships that will please God and be an asset to the ministry. He may decide to only send you one person or five – no matter the number – pray for friendships that will glorify God and bring each of you closer to Him as a result. No, they will not replace feelings of homesickness and missing your friends and family – but it will help you adapt and adjust more easily to your life away from home. It will give you the sense of community and family that you will need when you are faced with adversity and doubt.

Remember, there is no yellow brick road, no golden path. There is only the path that God has prepared for you – whatever that is, understand the pros and the cons and make a commitment to be faithful and fervent in your walk regardless. Pray for your husband, the congregation and yourself and ask God to send you friends that will support you, surround you and encourage you as you make the journey toward the unknown.

Prayer: *Lord, we don't always understand the path you've chosen for us, but we do know that You are always in total control. Teach us how to be faithful and fervent to what You have called us to do, even in our weakest moments when we feel alone and isolated. Give us the strength and faith to face our future with hope and promise and the knowledge that You are always there to care for us and to carry our burdens. As we face the unknowns in our lives, help us to cling to what we do know – that You are our comforter, our protection and our salvation! Amen.*

FIRST LADY: THE REAL TRUTH

CHAPTER 5

²⁹Let no corrupt communication proceed out of your mouth, but that which is good to the use of edifying, that it may minister grace unto the hearers. ³⁰And grieve not the holy Spirit of God, whereby ye are sealed unto the day of redemption. ³¹Let all bitterness, and wrath, and anger, and clamour, and evil speaking, be put away from you, with all malice: ³²And be ye kind one to another, tenderhearted, forgiving one another, even as God for Christ's sake hath forgiven you. ¹Be ye therefore followers of God, as dear children; ²And walk in love, as Christ also hath loved us, and hath given himself for us an offering and a sacrifice to God for a sweetsmelling savour. Ephesians 4:29-32;5:1-2

An invitation to the party: Avoiding the pity party when things don't go right

I f you don't already know, you will soon discover that the life of a pastor's wife can be filled with some very challenging times. There will be times when you will want to pack your things and get out of dodge on the first plane to anywhere! Someone might say something to you totally out of line, someone might attack your character or rise against your husband in absolute disrespect. You become angry and resentful and cry out "what's it all for?" You begin to wonder why you gave up your life, your family, to come to minister to people who don't appreciate you, who act like they don't want you there? You begin to question the call – is this really the place the Lord wants us? Maybe we should have waited and gone somewhere else. Maybe we should have stayed back home – at least we would have the support of those who love us. Why all this opposition when we are trying to do what we believe God has called us to do? Before you know it, you're hosting the biggest, grandest pity party that's ever been thrown! And you are at the center of the party, dressed in all your royal pitifulness and adorned with a face of scorn! You've made up in your mind one of two things, either 1) I'm not going back or 2) I'm not going to do anything in this church anymore!

Yes, can't you tell I've been there? I've hosted a few of these parties myself and have even invited others to join in the festivities! There have been times when I felt unwanted and unappreciated, and I made up my mind not to go back. Those times usually only lasted a few Sundays – because something within me won't allow me to miss worship! Then there were the times when I said I wasn't going to do anything! No ministry, nothing! "If they don't want me here, then I'll just sit back and do nothing!" was my attitude. Once I even retreated to the balcony, refusing to sit in my usual area – just to isolate myself from the pain I was feeling! I even had the nerve to invite someone else to join me in the balcony, and she did until she got tired of climbing those steps! I felt like a wounded puppy, but I returned to my seat after the Lord dealt with me about a few things: 1) Who was I serving? 2) What was my calling? and, 3) You can't get mad at man and quit on God!

Who was I serving? Jesus Christ! The One who before the beginning of time thought it not robbery to go to a rugged cross on my behalf, although I was so undeserving! The One who saved me from a life of sin and protected me from the streets of Philadelphia, although I had a drug-addicted mother and no father! The One who loved me enough to give me a husband that would love and cherish me unconditionally regardless of my issues and baggage! The One who blessed my womb and trusted me to mother two beautiful daughters, even though I didn't have the best examples of motherhood! The One who entrusted me with His Word to teach to other women, even though I felt inadequate and unworthy!!! This is the wonderful, powerful, omnipotent, omniscient, omnipresent God that I serve! Not man!

What was my calling? God called me to be a helpmeet to the man of God! Me, a poor little girl from West Philadelphia! I was to provide help and comfort to the man who would preach and teach God's Holy and Divine Word. I was to stand beside him and encourage him. I was to also use the gifts and talents that God had purposed in me to edify His people. I was to be an example of His grace and His mercy and to minister to the needs of others through my life and my experiences.

I can't get mad at man and quit on God. My husband says this all the time, and the words traveled from my head to my heart! Man didn't save me; man didn't call me and man can't call the shots concerning me! God is interested in how we respond to our dilemmas and our trials. Our response shows what we think about God, his hand on our lives, and our level of faith in Him.

When we are faced with these challenges, we must watch

our mouths and what we allow to escape from our lips. Ephesians 4:29 says, "Let no corrupt communication proceed out of your mouth, but that which is good to the use of edifying, that it may minister grace unto the hearers." Be careful what you say even to those that are closest to you. Your response in the midst of trouble will be an example of the grace that God has bestowed in your life. Then be careful not to grieve the Holy Spirit because you have responded in a negative and damaging way. Let the bitterness, wrath and anger, evil speaking – be put away from you. Yes, you may be justified in being upset or angry- but sin not. Let your response not be a sinful one – but one that is kind, tenderhearted and forgiving even as Christ has forgiven you! Remember that the congregation that you are a part of is God's people and therefore, His responsibility. Whatever He needs to do in and through their lives, He will do. He does not need you to host any pity parties, tell folks off, or get mad at them and want to quit ministry. He is not only trying to do a work in their lives, but He is also trying to do a work in yours! Be open to every challenge as you seek to find out what it is that God is pruning or perfecting in you! Then you can walk in love and be as Christ, a sacrifice that is a sweet smelling-savor unto the Lord! It's not easy, but through Christ, it's more than possible!

Prayer: *Lord, there are times in our lives when we admit that we want to give up. There is opposition when we try to do your will and our first response seems to be a fleshly one. We*

want to respond the way You want us to – with love and kindness, knowing that it is You who have called us to our positions. Please give us the courage, the wisdom and the power that is needed to overcome our challenges and continue what You have called us to do. Amen.

FIRST LADY: THE REAL TRUTH

CHAPTER 6

[3]The aged women likewise, that they be in behaviour as becometh holiness, not false accusers, not given to much wine, teachers of good things; [4]That they may teach the young women to be sober, to love their husbands, to love their children, [5]To be discreet, chaste, keepers at home, good, obedient to their own husbands, that the word of God be not blasphemed. Titus 2:3-5

Building relationships within the church: Relational ministry – A non-traditional approach

" Candie, this is great! You are building relationships with these women, many pastor's wives can't do that. You are blessed." The comment came from a very dear friend of mine (more like a mother!) when she came to Birmingham to visit for the weekend. Our women's ministry wanted to greet her and make her feel welcomed so we all got together and fixed dinner for my guest. We laughed and fellowshipped and had a wonderful time. Her words stayed with me because I never really thought that what I was doing was so unusual. I began to think about all of the pastor's wives that I knew and it began to dawn on me that it was a bit unusual. Many pastor's wives are disconnected from the other women in their congregation, for various reasons obviously. Our women's ministry meets at my home once a month. After having a few meetings at the church, we collectively thought that meeting at the church made our meetings more austere and impersonal, so we decided on a more intimate setting. We begin each meeting by fellowshipping over dinner and then I share God's Word with them. It is a very interactive and open atmosphere and over the span of the four years we've met, we have not only, with God's guidance, created a great women's ministry, we've created a wonderful sisterhood! We've been there for one another through some very trying times – we've fasted, we've prayed, we've encouraged, we've admonished – we have loved one another with a love that only God could give a roomful of women! We've also taken time to meet outside of our regular meetings, by going out to dinner together, having pajama parties in the winter and other fun activities that help us get to know one another better.

This chapter is not meant to encourage you to do women's ministry in your home, or to admonish you if you don't. Because, quite frankly, there are plenty of pastors out there who would say, "NO WAY!" My goal, however, is to let you see the importance of relational ministry – whether it is God's plan for you to minister to *one* or to one hundred! Being a pastor's wife has to be about more than just you! It has to be about more than you sitting on the first row and wearing white on First Sunday. There are so many people watching you – and some of them actually want to learn from you and your experiences! Are you a savior for the masses? No! But you can allow God to use you to grow someone else's faith while He develops yours.

I don't consider myself a very private person – but that's just me. I am not afraid for others to see my frailties and my inadequacies. A lot of my spiritual growth has been very public. I told you about my pity parties and balcony experience! Is that embarrassing? A little. But ultimately God gets the glory because then others can see God working in and through me. If I haven't understood anything else in my Christian walk, I've learned this "It's not about me!" We go through many times for someone else's benefit down the line! I feel I would do my sisters in Christ a disservice if I acted as if I never go through anything. Does this mean you tell all of your business and air out all your issues? No, that's not what I'm saying. However, don't get so caught up in the title of being "first lady" that you cannot minister to the needs of anyone else.

Relational ministry is just that – it's about relationships. Take some time to mentor someone. When we disciple other women and they are brought into maturity in Christ, we are availing ourselves to kingdom building! What experiences have you had that God can use to build up someone else? The position of pastor's wife doesn't have to mean that you are just a figure head – "his" wife, "their" mother, unapproachable and plastic. If women's ministry is not your calling or your passion, just concentrate on ministering in your circle of influence. You might be in a position to minister to other pastors' wives – Lord, knows that's needed! Consider creating a fellowship for other pastors' wives in your area. Create an atmosphere wherein pastors' wives feel safe and accepted.

There are many sisters across the country that is realizing that pastor's wives need support and mentoring. There are now conferences and workshops specifically for pastors' wives, for instance the First Lady Conferences by Lois Evans, wife to Pastor Tony Evans. If this interests you, get involved and begin to build relationships. Or, just ask the Lord to send you one sister you can help. She may be someone in the church whom you've known and watched struggle for years, or she may be a new convert, it doesn't matter. There are women in our churches who are hurting, confused and sinking and in need of comfort, friendship and personal attention. You don't have to have all the answers to her problems – but you have to be willing to listen and to love her and to sow God's Word into her heart. When the Lord raises that sister up she will, in turn, pay it forward to someone else and the cycle continues as the Church continues its mandate (Matt. 28:19,20).

Within our ministry we've tried to make it so that each woman is connected to someone else. We won't all be the best of friends collectively, but in groups of two or more we can stay connected and hold one another accountable. When the group needs to respond to someone collectively, then we all make ourselves available. This has been a great process, although we admit that we must make tremendous efforts to make it even greater!

Titus 2 says that in order to have a sound church there should be qualities associated with each group within the body. The mature women, through their reverent behavior, should lead the younger women. They should instruct them to love their husbands and children – be discreet, chaste, homemakers, good, obedient to their husbands – that the Word of God not be blasphemed. Can we do this effectively without building relationships? Do we, ourselves, listen to those whom we do not know? Jesus, himself, understood the importance of relationships. He didn't just meet up with his disciples on the Sabbath and spew out a bunch of instructions as to how they should live. He walked with them, he ate with them, he fellowshipped with them. He loved them enough to get personal with them.

Whatever your approach is to discipling others, be it traditional or non-traditional, step out on faith and make a difference in the life of someone else.

Prayer: *Lord, teach me how to sow into someone else's life Your wonderful Word and Your awesome precepts. Teach me how to come out of myself enough to build lasting and beneficial relationships with the women you have placed in my life so that they will be edified and that You will be glorified! Amen.*

FIRST LADY: THE REAL TRUTH

CHAPTER 7

⁶Now godliness with contentment is great gain. ⁷For we brought nothing into this world, and it is certain we can carry nothing out. ⁸And having food and clothing, with these we shall be content. ⁹But those who desire to be rich fall into temptation and a snare, and into many foolish and harmful lusts which drown men in destruction and perdition. ¹⁰For the love of money is a root of all kinds of evil, for which some have strayed from the faith in their greediness, and pierced themselves through with many sorrows. ¹¹But you, O man of God, flee these things and pursue righteousness,

godliness, faith, love, patience, gentleness. I Timothy 6:6-11

Focusing on the high calling:
It's not a competition

I often feel that the best part of ministry is being a lay person. When I look back to the years that my husband and I spent in church before he became a minister, and definitely before he became a pastor, those to me, were the best years of our lives together. We had a great church, filled with great people and we all basically wanted the same thing: to worship the Lord and be involved in ministry. We had a group of couples who were all newly married and beginning families and we fellowshipped and encouraged one another. Those were the good old days!

Then it all began to change almost drastically. Once my husband became a minister and ultimately a pastor a lot of our relationships began to change. It almost seems as if you are suddenly placed in a separate world. Some of the people you thought you were close to are no longer calling and your life changes forever! I haven't really put a finger on why that happens – perhaps it is God's way of weeding out certain people in your life or perhaps its Satan's way of isolating you so that he can distract you from your purpose. The jury is still out on that, although it's my suspicion that there is a little bit of both of these dynamics at work.

Life on "the other side of the pulpit" as I call it, is quite different. You are, more often than not, put in situations where you will be surrounded by other preachers and their wives and you begin to notice some things. Instead of what you might think will be a great network of preachers and their wives with whom you can fellowship and encourage one another, you might begin to hear conversations that are troublesome at best. Who has the largest church, who's getting paid the most money, who has the most things - cars, homes, who's a better preacher, who's church has the most ministries.....and the list goes on. Oh, didn't you know? Preachers are people too. And that's not to say that this talk goes on with all preachers. I know a lot of preachers who are sincere, who are concerned about ministry and God's people and who could care less who has a 7:30 a.m. and an 11:00 a.m. worship service! If you find these preachers and their wives, stick to them like glue!

My point in this chapter is to encourage you and your spouse to concentrate and stay focused on what it is the Lord has called you to do. Don't let the devil and others convince you that ministry is a competition – because it isn't.

I know we're living in the mega church era – but everyone is not called to pastor a mega church, nor will every smaller church become a mega church! You can have all of the conferences and seminars you want on how to grow your church into a mega church, but God has placed you where He wants you and the church will only grow to the size HE has ordained it to be. Am I saying don't strive to increase the size of your church by biblical methods? No, I'm saying don't get so caught up in the size of a church that you are no longer being productive and effective for the Lord, but rather you and your spouse are preoccupied with being rich and well known locally or nationally!

It is a sad day for Christianity if the conception out there is that the ministry of the Gospel is equated with riches, prosperity and affluence and not with the saving grace of a loving and spectacular Savior! Is it wrong for a minister of the gospel to be affluent? No, definitely not. However, it should not be the intent of anyone to purposely go into ministry with the idea that they will receive riches, power and fame.

My husband's first church was very small and we watched as others around us seemed to prosper in their larger congregations. I have to admit that I had a hard time watching as some pastors prospered with gimmicks and tricks to increase their memberships. They rode around in expensive cars and wore the finest of clothes as my husband struggled to pay our daughters' school tuition.

However, we remained focused and committed to our task. Arthur relentlessly preached God's Word as if we had a standing room only crowd every Sunday and I continued to do women's ministry whether I had one person or fifty!

We must learn to be content with what God has given us! Whether he blesses your husband in a congregation of five thousand, five hundred, or fifty, you both have to be content where he places you and stay focused on the high calling He has upon your lives. Please trust that I'm not saying that there is any thing wrong with having a large congregation, my home church is, in my opinion, a mega church. However, as the body of believers we must understand that God does not bless all of us alike but that doesn't mean that we should begin to covet someone else's blessings and not stop until we have what they have. We won't all have a T. D. Jakes or an Eddie Long ministry – but we must invest in the ministry that God has given us, no matter how large or small, with the same vigor, power and excellence.

It is not, however, easy being content when you have unmet needs. If your spouse is teaching and preaching God's Word with all his might and the church is struggling to supply even your basic needs, of course you will feel a bit of angst. However, God wants to teach us how to be content with the means we have, the church He's placed us in, the families we have, etc. This shows Him that we trust in His leadership, in His guiding hand. It doesn't mean He'll never change our circumstances, nor does it mean that we can't pursue ways to better our situation, after all His word tells us that we can do all things through Him who strengthens us (Phil. 4: 13). Previous to that verse, Paul says that he has learned how to be content –to abound and to be abased. Many times God will wait to bless us with more after such time as we have proved that we are grateful and can handle what we already have.

We must consistently seek to improve in the areas of our lives that God reveals to us need work. The scripture tells us to pursue righteousness, godliness, faith, love, patience, gentleness – it does not tell us to seek to have the biggest and best church, to seek to have riches and infamy, to have the most ministries. We have more than enough examples of what happens to the man of God when he seeks after these things, rather than the riches of God's Word and to be a servant to His people. Remember that these actions do not just affect the man of God, but also his family. If your spouse embraces this type of attitude – to be rich and famous –rather than to be used by God for His purpose – then your responsibility is to pray on his behalf that God would open his eyes and his heart and return him to his first love so that he may, "Preach the word; be instant in season, out of season; reprove, rebuke, exhort with all long suffering and doctrine. (2 Timothy 4:2). Paul instructed Timothy to reprove (convince), rebuke and exhort – with longsuffering and teaching. Have you ever tried to convince someone of something? Were you not passionate about what you were saying? Didn't you make sure that you had all of your facts and information correct so that you appeared knowledgeable about the subject? The man of God has to stay focused and dependant upon God's Word in order to convince others of its saving power! Paul told Timothy when they no longer want to hear the sound doctrine – you still must be watchful in all things, endure afflictions, do the work of an evangelist, and fulfill your ministry!

Those instructions don't sound very glamorous to me! Watchful and endure afflictions? Afflictions? What afflictions? Yes, there will be many afflictions. Just think about it. What happens when you say things that people don't want to hear? Do they bombard you with gifts and tell you how wonderful you are? Do they invite you over and treat you like gold? Absolutely not! They talk about you, they despise you, they alienate you and more! That's the real part of ministry that must be understood. Will the people like you and your husband when it seems he won't give them a little bit of "sugar" with the Gospel? When his messages don't make them comfortable? Paul told Timothy to fulfill his ministry! That means that regardless of whether or not you are received, regardless of whether or not you are appreciated, or whether you and your spouse get to live in a huge house or drive the latest car – you must fulfill your ministry. If these creature comforts never happen for you – will you still devote your lives to the ministry? It is important to realize that those you see on television are the minority not the majority! There are millions of preachers and their families, whose names you will never know, that have given their lives for the furtherance of the Gospel. There are missionaries in Third World countries that are living in huts among natives so that they can spread God's Word!

Your motives must be clear when you set out on this journey called ministry! If you are blessed to be in a situation where you are compensated generously –then praise God! The Bible says that a man is worthy of his hire. However, even in that be humble and don't forget the message! The message is never to be about you and what you have – it must always point directly to Jesus!

If the Lord sends your spouse and you to a large congregation or grows your congregation to a larger size, continue to stay focused and don't get caught up in these silly comparisons and competitions. Remember that it is not "Your" church, but that it is God's church and that He must have the final say over every decision and every aspect of the church's future. Be humble, be committed and be charitable! Find a smaller church to help. If you see a pastor and his congregation struggling and your church can help, partner up with them and help them with their ministry. Larger churches shouldn't exist to stand alone and be looked up to. Our goals should be common: to exalt Jesus Christ, win the lost and edify the saints of God. We should be able to do that as ONE body in Christ – not divided by size, annual budgets or preaching styles! Remember it's not a competition – but a High Calling!

Prayer: *Lord, no matter the size of the congregation you have placed us in, Help us to be committed to the High*

Calling you have given us. Help us not to be caught up in silly comparisons that further divide the Body of Christ, but that we would embrace all of our brothers and sisters in Christ and unite together in pursuing righteousness and winning souls for your kingdom. Amen.

FIRST LADY: THE REAL TRUTH

CHAPTER 8

[1]Wives, likewise, be submissive to your own husbands, that even if some do not obey the word, they, without a word, may be won by the conduct of their wives, [2]when they observe your chaste conduct accompanied by fear. [3]Do not let your adornment be merely outward—arranging the hair, wearing gold, or putting on fine apparel— [4]rather let it be the hidden person of the heart, with the incorruptible beauty of a gentle and quiet spirit, which is very precious in the sight of God. [5]For in this manner, in former times, the holy women who trusted in God also adorned themselves, being submissive to their own husbands, [6]as Sarah obeyed Abraham, calling him lord, whose daughters you are if you do good and are not afraid with any terror.[7]Husbands, likewise, dwell with them with understanding, giving honor to the wife, as to the weaker vessel, and as being heirs together of the grace of life, that your prayers may not be hindered.[8]Finally, all of you be of one mind, having compassion for one another; love as brothers, be tenderhearted, be courteous; [9]not returning evil for evil or reviling for reviling, but on the contrary blessing, knowing that you were called to this, that you may inherit a blessing. I Peter 3:1-10

Peace in the valley: Dealing with the man of God when he is in sin

We mentioned earlier the significance of submission in marriage. It is vital that the wife adorn herself with gentleness and godliness so that she can be the wife that God desires. However, the Bible also clearly describes the desired characteristics of the husband. I Peter says that he is to be understanding, that he is to honor her so that his prayers be not hindered. These instructions denote a connection between how a man treats his wife and his answers to prayer. It suggests that if he does not treat his spouse with understanding and honor, then his prayers will be hindered which shows a break in fellowship with the Father.

So what then to the many situations in which the man of God is disobeying these instructions? I've interviewed many women across the country that have horrifying accounts of neglect, abuse (both physical and mental), adultery and more! What should the response be to such blatant disregard for the purpose of marriage, especially by the man of God?

I won't pretend to have the answer to that question! I'm not a psychiatrist or a counselor and I don't even play one on t.v. However, I will say that there a number of responses that I know for sure!

If you are in a dangerous situation in which your life is in jeopardy, I advise you to GET OUT!!! I don't believe that God is calling us to remain in relationships that threaten our lives! Any woman – whether married to a pastor or not – should get out from under physical abuse! Remember those biblical instances such as when Saul wanted to take David's life, David didn't stay –the Lord made a way of escape for him! After you have removed yourself from such a dangerous situation, you should contact the appropriate law enforcement and social agencies for further assistance. I would suggest that you immediately connect with your fellow saints of God that will give you sound, biblical, advice and support. Do not listen to those who will tell you to "think about his career and the church." Your life is more important than his needs at this point, especially if there are children involved.

What should be the advice for women who are hurting in their marriages to pastors because of infidelity, neglect and other issues? I cannot give first hand advice because that has not been my story. I do, however, think it is important to have this discussion as there are many women who are faced with this reality every day. We have a habit of putting sin into categories. We usually ascribe to the sins of infidelity and abuse as being "big sins" that we cannot live with and sins like dishonesty, neglect, selfishness, etc. as "smaller sins" that we may choose to live with. Well, the reality is that sin is sin. No matter how you categorize them, if the husband doesn't "dwell with understanding, give honor to the wife as to the weaker vessel, and as being heirs together of the grace of life", then his prayers will be hindered and he is out of the will of God!

It is so important that all of us, as Christians, have someone else to whom we are accountable to! There ought to be someone in your and your husband's circle of Christian friends that can give you sound, biblical advice and that are not afraid to rebuke your actions when you are out of God's will! I don't care large your church is or how important your husband is, or even how well known he is across the globe! If your husband is in sin (we're talking about a habitual state of sin- because we all are guilty of sin), then it is critical that someone hold him accountable. Your pastor or one of his fellow preachers of the Gospel should be able to confront him in love. If he truly desires to be in fellowship with the Lord and with you, he will listen and seek to correct his behavior.

Recently, a well known minister of the Gospel fell into sin and his story was blasted in the media. I don't have the authority to judge this minister or his actions, but I was impressed by how it was handled by the ministry he belonged to. They rallied together and made teams of men to whom he had to be accountable to and provided for him the counseling necessary for him and his wife to heal and recover. Isn't this our responsibility to one another? In the next verses of I Peter it says, "Finally, all of you be of one mind, having compassion for one another, love as brothers, be tenderhearted, be courteous." We have a responsibility to one another. It should be the intent of every married Christian couple, whether in ministry or not, to cultivate relationships with other couples so that if the time ever arises, you will be there for one another to correct, rebuke and exhort! As a matter of fact, if we have these buffers in place BEFORE the need arises, the need might, in fact, NEVER arise!

When the man of God is in sin, he is not above correction! Your response as a wife, however, should be that of gentleness, prayer and sincere love. If you cannot reach him yourself, you should go in prayer that the Lord will provide the appropriate person to approach him – be that his pastor or a trusted friend and you must continue to love him unconditionally as he is restored to a right relationship with Christ and with you. This is easier said than done when you have been the victim of his actions, but it is not impossible! If there are circumstances in which trust has been broken and pain has been constant, then you both should seek marriage counseling from an impartial Christian counselor to restore your relationship. You do not have the power to change your spouse, as we stated earlier, however, your response to the situation is critical so be prayerful and sensitive to God's guidance.

Prayer: *Lord, I pray right now for the covering of the Holy Spirit on my mate. Please protect him from the temptations and snares of the devil that are designed to keep him out of fellowship with You and me. Give us friends and confidants that love You and that will embrace us when we go through, but that will not be afraid to correct, rebuke or exhort us into a right relationship with You! Amen.*

FIRST LADY: THE REAL TRUTH

CHAPTER 9

⁴Then the word of the LORD came unto me, saying, ⁵Before I formed thee in the belly I knew thee; and before thou camest forth out of the womb I sanctified thee, and I ordained thee a prophet unto the nations. ⁶Then said I, Ah, Lord GOD! Behold, I cannot speak: for I am a child. ⁷But the LORD said unto me, Say not, I am a child: for thou shalt go to all that I shall send thee, and whatsoever I command thee thou shalt speak. ⁸Be not afraid of their faces: for I am with thee to deliver thee, saith the LORD. ⁹Then the LORD put forth his hand, and touched my mouth. And the LORD said unto me, Behold, I have put my words in thy mouth. Jeremiah 1:4-9 ³⁷ Turn away my eyes from looking at worthless things, *And* revive me in Your way. (NKJV) ³⁷Turn away my eyes from beholding vanity (idols and idolatry); and restore me to vigorous life and health in Your ways. (AMP) Psalm 119:37

The "L" word: Loneliness in a church full of folk!

It almost sounds like an oxymoron, right? How can you be lonely in a church full of people? And when I say "church full", it doesn't necessarily speak to specific numbers of people within your congregation. No matter the size of the congregation, it is certainly a possibility that you and your spouse will experience loneliness as a couple and/or as individuals.

For some, the pastor's family is looked at as "employees" of the church. Therefore, you and your spouse might be called upon only if there is a need or crisis in the congregation. You might not be included in personal events or get invitations to Christmas dinner or to share in the lives of the members. Therefore, you may never feel as if you have a "relationship" with the people. On the other hand, you may get all the invitations in the world – yet still feel disconnected or as if you don't quite "fit in" with members of the congregation. The life of the pastor's wife can be complicated. So how do you deal with this life if you, in fact, are one of the ones that feel lonely in a church full of folks?

You may not have found someone with whom to associate with on a personal level – someone who is not around you for any ulterior motives or is not constantly judging you, but is rooting for you and praying with you. What if you are not accepted by the congregation other than to "serve" and each Sunday you feel like an "outsider" who has just been invited to the party because of who you know (which is, in this case, your spouse)?

First, don't get me wrong, I don't think that the pastor and his wife should be "personal" with everyone in the congregation. Personally, I think it's a good thing if they aren't. This allows for total objectivity and non-bias decision making within the congregation. However, you need to understand that the Lord can send you and your spouse specific people within the congregation with whom you can fellowship on a personal level. But….what if He chooses not to? Suppose you are, as we stated in previous chapters, away from your hometown and the Lord doesn't place anyone within the congregation in your lives to accept you or fellowship with you outside the duties of your roles and positions? Or suppose you are in a church that has shown you that they appreciate not just what you do for them, but who you are as an individual – yet you still are plagued by the "L" word? I was able to pull some things from our opening scripture in Jeremiah that helped me to get over the "L" word (or at least get past it when Satan tries to use it to isolate me). But first, I must say two things. One, remember that the "L" word is about how you are *feeling*. Two, remember that Satan loves to turn what you are "feeling" into something so big that it isolates you or hinders you from seeing what God is really doing in your life. Regarding loneliness, we must look inward to ensure that we are not causing our own isolation. Have you made yourself available? The Bible says to have friends we must show ourselves friendly. Do people get the impression that they can approach you, or are you stand-offish and so self-centered that people don't want to have anything to do with you? Make sure that you are not exhibiting any type of behavior that would exclude you from building relationships within the congregation.

However, when you've done all you can to be accessible and approachable and you still feel lonely or like you're on the sidelines looking in – two things have to be realized, but ultimately God is still in control of the situation.

One realization you must consider about the loneliness you feel is that whatever need for comfort, fellowship or acceptance you are seeking may not be met within the congregation anyway (or at least it may be delayed by God's timing). If this is the case, then it brings me to the other point: instead of concentrating on the void you *feel* within the congregation, begin to fill it with the other things that God has called you to do.

God had a job for Jeremiah to do. He needed Jeremiah to relay a message to Judah about their disobedience and their callous disregard toward Him. Jeremiah preached and prophesied that message for 40 years. Judah didn't want to hear it! They ignored, rejected, and persecuted Jeremiah for his stance on the sin in their lives, but eventually they experienced God's judgment because they didn't take heed to Jeremiah's message. However, when God initially told Jeremiah what he was to do, he felt insecure and unsure. Out of this conversation between Jeremiah and God, I was comforted. Three things helped me to deal with loneliness while in the midst of a church full of folks and I was able to counteract the "L" word with some "L" words of my own: *listen, lean, and love*.

Listen

Learn to listen to God! God told Jeremiah that He had sanctified (set him apart) for service even before he was placed in his mother's womb! God set you and your spouse apart for exclusive use when you were just a concept in His mind! You weren't even a reality for your mother when God was making plans for your life! He has set you aside for a job, learn how to listen to His guidance. When you are listening to God, you are not focusing or concentrating on whether or not others are accepting you. Yes, you may notice it – but you're not focused on it! It doesn't become a part of your spirit so much so that you begin to be bitter or consumed by it. The only sure way to listen to God is to spend time with Him. Make sure that you are spending quality time in prayer and study of God's Word. This is crucial! Time spent with the Lord makes it harder for Satan to penetrate your spirit and fill you with feelings of loneliness and depression. That's not to say that you won't experience them or that he won't penetrate, but it does make it harder for him! God can fill any void you may feel and He wants you to discuss your feelings with Him so that He can not only comfort you, but guide you as well.

Lean

Lean on God! He told Jeremiah that He was the One who sent him – that He would be with him and deliver him and so He is with you. The Bible tells us to cast our cares upon Him because He cares for us. He cares about everything that concerns us and everything that we are facing. He has not sent us to do ministry to leave us to our own devices. Remember that wherever God has placed you and your spouse – that He, is the One in fact, that placed you there. With God's vision comes provision! He will be with you and He is working everything out for your good.

I like verse 6 that says, "don't be afraid of their faces". Don't worry about not being accepted (whatever that means for you). Don't worry about the looks of disdain or the cold shoulders you might experience. God is the One that has set your life on this path. Jeremiah was rejected and the people didn't want to hear him, but he kept delivering the message. Continue to do what God has called you to do. Continue to support your husband. Continue to support the ministry. Continue to fulfill your purpose. Don't mope around about what you're not getting or complaining about who doesn't like you. Like the old folks used to say, "You've got a charge to keep and a God to glorify." There isn't any time to nurture the "L" word. Let it go and go on. How, you say? That brings us to our next point:

Love

In the midst of what you are *feeling,* you can choose to love using God's language. What does that mean? Verse 9 says, "⁹Then the LORD put forth his hand, and touched my mouth. And the LORD said unto me, Behold, I have put my words in thy mouth." The Lord has put His words in your mouth! Allow only those words to come out of your mouth. Watch your tongue and take your tongue off of God's people! Did you get that? Take YOUR tongue off of God's people. I had to repeat that so that I, myself, could get that in my spirit! The people that God has sent to the church at which your husband serves, are HIS people. Regardless of the angst you might be experiencing, regardless of the pain they may have caused you, regardless of the isolation you might feel – they are HIS people and your responsibility is to love and pray for them. So, stop using negative language about them – stop speaking out of your pain and start speaking God's love language. You may not be saying the negative things to them per se (or I don't know, maybe some of you are!), but you're saying them to your spouse, to your girlfriend, to your momma! Take your tongue off of them and allow the Lord to soothe your tongue with His Word. If anything can change the situation that you are in the midst of, it is the Word of God! I heard a speaker say once that when we internalize something it travels from our minds to our hearts and eventually comes out of our mouth. Begin to attack those negative words when they enter your mind so that they won't fester in your heart and come out of your mouth!

Vanity

You might be wondering how the final scripture in this chapter is connected to our discussion.

³⁷ Turn away my eyes from looking at worthless things, *And* revive me in Your way. (NKJV)

³⁷Turn away my eyes from beholding vanity (idols and idolatry); and restore me to vigorous life and health in Your ways.

(AMP)

Recently, I had really begun to feel a sense of loneliness and I couldn't quite put my finger on what was going wrong or what, if anything, I had done to feel this way. It seemed that some people in my life were beginning to literally disappear. Friendships that I thought were in place were now jeopardized and the numbers of trusted friends were diminishing. I couldn't understand it. I had not, I felt, done anything to isolate anyone. If I had, it was not made known to me. So, I was beginning to feel lonely and isolated until I began to do a study on Psalm 119. A friend told me about a series that Sis. Gordon was doing on the chapter and I decided to follow along in my own personal devotion. It was the right move at the right time!

Although I love the entire book, one specific verse hit me upside my head and I found myself repeating it daily and that is verse 37. The KJV says, "37Turn away mine eyes from beholding vanity; and quicken thou me in thy way." But I, personally, love the NKJV which says, "Turn away my eyes from looking at worthless things." Where was this need coming from to be accepted by others? Was it loneliness or vanity? Did I think that I was so great that surely others would want to befriend me? Was it pride? I'm not exactly sure what the cause or the root of the feeling – but I do know one thing! God was telling me to turn my eyes away from it because in the scheme of His plan for my life – it was worthless!!!! It didn't mean anything! It neither added nor took away anything from my purpose – so I needed to turn away from it! Literally, stop looking at it!!!

What did I want from the Lord instead? To revive me in His way! To restore me to vigorous life and health!

Whatever you are looking at, are focusing on, are dwelling on – that is causing you to feel down, isolated or depressed – or WHOEVER your looking at - turn your eyes away from it and look to Jesus – the author and finisher of your faith! If you are caught up in the vanity of your own mind – if you are placing other things, other people, or even yourself (idolatry) in front of the plans God has for you – turn away from these worthless things and be restored today! This scripture helped me tremendously get over myself and move on. Sometimes the Lord has people in your lives for only a season! There are people that will be there for a short time, then there are people that will be there for a lifetime! But, he knows what's best for you. If you know that you haven't offended or misused the friendship of another – take your hands off of it and allow the Lord to do His thing! He may be moving the person out of your life to make way for another one. He may be changing the type of relationship you have with another. I like what Tyler Perry said in a few of his films/plays, "Sometimes we are trying to keep together what God, Himself, is trying to tear apart."

What or who are you fixated on? Is it friendships, is it feelings, is it you??? Once you realize that EVERYTHING outside of Christ is worthless, you can experience the joy and happiness of the Lord! That means that nothing has worth, unless God is in it! Ask God to reveal to you what those worthless things are that you are focusing on – and then ask Him to help you turn away your eyes from it and restore you to the vigorous and healthy life that He has prepared just for you!

I guarantee that if you begin to listen to God, lean on Him and use his love language, and turn your eyes away from the worthless things that try to vie for your attention, it will bring you closer to fulfilling the purpose that He has for you and you won't have any time for the "L" word!

Prayer: *Lord, we know that being in ministry is not easy. There may even be times when we feel isolated and lonely. However, we can rest assure that you have called us, sanctified us, and put Your Word in our mouths. Teach us how to listen to You through your Word, how to lean on You and how to constantly use your love language – when speaking about Your people that You have called us to serve. And teach us how to turn our eyes away*

from any worthless thing that tries to hinder us from fulfilling Your purpose for our lives. Amen.

FIRST LADY: THE REAL TRUTH

CHAPTER 10

[8]And above all things have fervent love for one another, for "love will cover a multitude of sins." [9]*Be* hospitable to one another without grumbling. [10]As each one has received a gift, minister it to one another, as good stewards of the manifold grace of God. [11]If anyone speaks, *let him speak* as the oracles of God. If anyone ministers, *let him do it* as with the ability which God supplies, that in all things God may be glorified through Jesus Christ, to whom belong the glory and the dominion forever and ever. Amen. I Peter 4:8-11

A purpose fulfilled:
Resting in your role as pastor's wife

If anyone had told me years ago that I would be a pastor's wife, I would have laughed in their face! Being a pastor's wife had never once crossed my mind as I pondered my future! To be quite honest, when I was dating, I purposely avoided anyone associated with the preaching ministry. When Arthur and I dated he was a Sunday School teacher and active in youth ministry, that didn't bother me. Had I known that he would be called into full-time ministry, I might have run the other way! However, after being in ministry with my husband for 17 years, I have come to grips with the fact that this is my role.

Do I still struggle with this lifestyle and want out? Oh, most definitely! There are times when I want it over with – when I want to live the life that I get to choose. How do you get past that feeling? By resting in your role as pastor's wife.

You have to come to terms with the fact that your life is not your own. God has purposed you and your spouse for such a time as this. He has given you a job to do and not only must you do it, but you must do it as unto the Lord.

This passage of scripture in I Peter sums up your responsibility not only to the congregation you serve, but also to the calling to which you've been called by the Lord.

What is your responsibility to God's people – the congregation? To love them fervently! The word fervently means passionately, enthusiastically, zealously, fanatically, excitedly. The opposite of fervently is indifferently! You must love that congregation with all of your being! WOW! That is a tough one! You and your spouse must love God's people with everything you've got because not to do so is to be indifferent which is to be uninterested, uncaring, unresponsive, and apathetic! The Word says that that kind of love will cover a multitude of sins! It didn't say only love them when they love you, love them when they support you, love them when they treat you right! It says love them fervently, period!

Be hospitable without grumbling! Don't complain about showing hospitality toward them even when they misuse you or are unappreciative. Trust me, you will battle with this one constantly!

Whatever it is that God has called you to do- however God has ordained for your mate to minister and whatever role you have in that ministry, be a good steward over your part and do it so that God is the one that gets the glory! In all things allow God to get the glory that is due His name!

You can rest in your role as pastor's wife, even if you didn't want it, even if it takes you out of your comfort zone, because you realize that this role is a part of God's purpose and plan for your life and your job is to give Him glory! You will find that you will have to constantly remind yourself of your purpose. It is not easy or comfortable or glamorous to be in the role of pastor's wife. For some it can be quite lonely, isolated and awkward, for others not so much, but the bottom line is that for none is it easy! The role may be quite ambiguous in today's churches, but as a woman of God with a purpose, it is quite clear of the pastor's wife's role, "that in all things God may be glorified through Jesus Christ, to whom belong the glory and the dominion forever and ever."

I encourage you as you seek to define what God's purpose is for you, that you support your mate, love God's people, be a good steward over the position and your home, and in all things give Him glory!

Prayer: *Lord, as I embark on my role as minister's/ pastor's wife, or as I continue to walk therein, please give me the strength to rest in my role as you have ordained. Please help me to support my mate, to fervently love your people, to be a good steward over the gifts and family that you have placed in my life, and in all things give you glory! Help me to accept my purpose and to trust you without wavering. Amen.*

ABOUT THE AUTHOR

As a writer and educator, Candie A. Mitchell-Price is committed to encouraging, inspiring, and empowering others toward a closer walk with Jesus Christ through her work. A proud native of Philadelphia, PA, Candie has authored two other books, He Restoreth My Soul and Straight Outta Brokenness, And It Didn't Kill Me. She is the Founder/Editor-in-Chief of WOW! (Women of the Word) Magazine, a national lifestyle magazine for Christian women which is returning in January, 2025 (wowmagazine.org).

Candie holds a BA in Communications Studies, specializing in Public Relations, and Masters degrees in Christian Education and Public Relations. A sought-after speaker, she has delivered talks at local and national women's retreats, conferences, and workshops.

She is married to Rev. Arthur Price, Jr., pastor of the historic 16th Street Baptist Church in Birmingham, AL. They are the proud parents of two adult children, Eboni Paige and Amyna Janel.

www.ingramcontent.com/pod-product-compliance
Lightning Source LLC
Chambersburg PA
CBHW060333130626
46553CB00003B/994